Table of Contents

Table of Contents 1

Preface 3

Get Organized 7

Priorities 9

Passion 21

Goal setting 25

Identifying Desired Job 33

Become an Expert 43

Volunteering 51

Education – Benefits vs. Expectations 59

Finances 65

Social Media 71

Self employment 75

Applications 79

Resume 87

Cover Letters 103

References 105

Researching possible employers 111

Looking for a Job 115

Interviewing 127

- Keeping Your job 137
- Conclusion 155
- Recommended Resources 157
- Biblical Perspective on Work 159

Preface

I believe that each person has something they can do, better than most others. Finding that "something" and putting it to good use is the key to enjoying what you are doing. For most people, money is not the only factor in choosing what they want to do with their life. They want a meaningful life. My hope is that this book will be a tool to help you find your passion, discover what you want to do with the next chapter of your life, and land your next job.

How many books have you read on how to look for a job? Truthfully, how many have you started reading? How many did you complete?

I have started many books (I don't know how many), but have finished only a few. Most of the books I finished were short and to the point. They had stories to which I could relate, or at least found interesting. These books had one other thing in common: I was able to use them as reference guides. After I finished a book, I was able to go back through it and look at the parts I needed, when I needed them.

This is what I hope this book is for you. I am trying to tell relevant stories so you will be able to learn from other people's mistakes (often my own) and, therefore, become wiser and better able to pursue your passions in the field in which you choose to work.

The style of this book is conversational on purpose. This is me sharing knowledge, ideas, and experiences with you.

If you are looking for a book to give you all the answers on any subject, this is not what you want. This book is intended to give you what you need to get started.

Throughout this book, you will find references to other books, including and especially the Bible. In my experience, the Bible has been proven to answer many of our questions, or to tell us what questions to ask. I am sure I have taken some Scripture out of context in order to make it meaningful in this document. I recommend that you review the context in which the verses reside, and if I have inappropriately quoted the verse, I apologize for the confusion.

Much of this book is written from a Christian perspective. While I tried to avoid preaching, there are times when a reference or statement is from that perspective. If you are not a Christian, please make sure you understand the reference or statement. It is applicable in some way, no matter what your background may be.

This book is written as a reference guide for a Job Networking group that can be part of a church ministry.

For more information about a Job Networking group or how to start one in your own church, please see our web site: www.HELPsperts.com under Job Networking. The questionnaires in this book are also available as downloads from our site. Please feel free to download them and utilize them to fit your needs.

As always, if you have questions, concerns, or suggestions regarding changes to anything in this book, please feel free to contact me at: book@HELPsperts.com.

I would like to express my gratitude to you for reading this book. My hope for you is that it will benefit you and those around you, and that you will be able to find your passion in your everyday life, especially at your job.

If you feel this book has helped you, please feel free to contact me at: Book@HELPsperts.com. Tell me your story. How has this book helped you? What would make it better?

Tim Van Norman

Get Organized

Beginning when you first decide you need a new job, until 6 months into the job, there are a number of things that you should know or at least think about.

Many people start their job search by putting together a resume and then trying to figure out what they want to do. This facilitates a job search that becomes disorganized and time consuming. While a job search is time consuming, it does not have to be disorganized.

In this book you will find an organized system to help you:

1. Identify the right job for you
2. Identify the companies you want to work for
3. Fill in gaps in your resume through volunteering
4. Write a resume
5. Write cover letters
6. Search for your desired job
7. Interview
8. Keep your job

Document your progress through a Job Search Log.

A Job Search Log is a document you will use to ensure you keep track of your job search. When performing a job search, you need to track what steps you have accomplished with each person and company with which you have interacted. This means that if you have sent a resume, your Job Search Log will have an entry for that company stating: which resume you sent, in response to which type of inquiry, and when you sent the resume. Later, you will also document any e-mails and phone calls to that company along with each person at the company with which you had contact.

Using a Job Search Log will help keep your spirits up while searching for a job. When you feel like you have done the same steps over and over, a Log will help you remember exactly where you are in the process with each company, and, therefore, what you can do to move to the next step. It also gives you the ability to document what you learned so you can apply it with the next company.

Follow the steps in the next chapters, in order, and you will have a very organized job search.

Priorities

What is your priority?

Notice, the question is not, what should your priority be; rather it is, "What is your priority?"

The following items should be on your priority list. They are listed here in no particular order:

- Faith
- Family
- Yourself
- Job
- Career

Notice in the above list, there is no mention of car, house, clothing, jewelry, money, etc. These material goods fall under one of the above categories. Also notice, "yourself" is a category. It is very important to know where you stand in your priority list.

When you define your priorities, you are better able to set goals and identify more clearly what type of job best fits you. For instance, if your family is a high priority, you may want a job that keeps you geographically close to your family or one that has you at home every night. Or, you may choose to look for a job that allows you to earn more money in order to put your children through school. Even though others may have the same priority order as you, this does not mean that it will be reflected in the same way.

As you continue in your career, you may find conflicts between your priorities. This is when you glimpse the real order of your priorities.

You need to identify what your priorities are. In order to set your Priority list, here is something you need to remember:

The Bible says, "where your treasure is, there your heart will be also."[1] This means that you will focus your attention on where your money is. In other words, where do you spend your money? Is it to take care of others? Your family? Your lifestyle? The environment? Your church? Another way of putting it is "Money talks". A quick note on why money is specifically not on this Priority list: Very few people earn money just to collect money. You earn money to enable you to do something or purchase something. The purchase could be food for your family, or a car for you. You could also earn money to be able to give to a cause you have faith in or provide a security net for you and your family. Money is not itself a priority.

Let's take a look at each of these priorities:

---

[1] Matthew 6:21, Luke 12:34

Faith

Faith includes church, spending time in creation, gaining an understanding of something greater than you. I am most familiar with the Christian faith, so these next statements may not seem appropriate if you are not a Christian; however, they do translate to whatever world view you may hold. Christians are taught to give to God and others. How willing are you to do so? This can be a measure of where faith fits in your priority list.

Outlets for this priority can include being involved in teaching others about God or spiritual matters, helping others, saving or beautifying buildings, the environment, or working with animals. This includes donating time and money to causes that you care about.

Family

Family includes your spouse, children, parents, extended family, and anyone else that you determine you are very close to. For some people family only includes "immediate family;" for others it can extend to close friends.

Based on whatever definition of family you have, where do they stand in your priority list? A priority of family, can mean visiting sick relatives instead of going to a ballgame. It could mean calling your elderly parents, or spending time at home instead of going to the gym.

Each person will demonstrate their priorities in a different way.

For many years, I found that I could not afford to be involved in activities that my kids were not involved in. This meant that I joined the board for Little League, taught Sunday School, and led Church youth groups. Basically, outside of work, I would only be involved in activities and organizations that would benefit my kids, or that they were involved in. My rationale was that this allowed me to be involved in my kids' lives and still provide the creative outlets I needed. These choices show how I put my family above myself in my priority list.

If you want to know where your family fits in your priority list, do this exercise:

- If _____ (fill in the blank with a family member's name) is sick,
    - Would I know?
    - Would I care?
    - Would I take time off work?
    - Would I take them to the doctor?
    - Would I sit in a doctor's office waiting for them?
    - Or would I not have the time to take care of this person.

Another question is, "If I have a decision to make quickly, that will affect my job or career, do I need to discuss that decision with my spouse, children, parents, etc.?"

The answer to these questions will help you determine where your family fits in your priority list.

Remember: Consciously identifying your priorities will help you make appropriate decisions.

Yourself

Some people feel that you should never have yourself as a priority. I COMPLETELY disagree. While I feel you should not have yourself as your highest priority, you MUST have yourself as a priority at some level. Some people show this priority by purchasing a house, car, boat, toy, etc. that they would really like to have. Other people show a lack of prioritizing themselves by not grooming themselves or not keeping up their personal appearance.

At this point, I would like to try to debunk some of the theories behind humility and the concept of being humble. In many circles, being humble is equated with being weak or self deprecating. NEITHER is accurate. The Bible says, "Do not think of yourself more highly than you ought."[2] Notice it does NOT say "Do not think of yourself." You have also heard "If you are proud, you

[2] Romans 12:3 b

will fall."[3] Some people feel that in these verses, the Bible is saying that you should not have pride nor should you think of yourself. Take a look at the last part of the first verse quoted, "more highly than he ought to think." This means that you need to know and understand yourself. Understand where you fit in the world as well as in your family and your job. It also is a reference to respecting others no matter what their position. Jesus had followers that were fishermen, tax collectors, as well as doctors. Each person was important, no matter what their position in the class structure. The same is true today. How well can a surgeon perform, if no one takes out the trash?

I try to consider the unwritten last line of my employment agreement to state "and anything else you are asked to do." What this means is that I consider my work responsibility to include anything else I am asked to do. This can mean dumping the trash or using a plunger on the toilet. It can mean being asked to lay off personnel even if I do not want to. Any task given to me is my responsibility. I have told each person who has worked for me, that I NEVER want to hear, "That is not my job," when I give them something to do. Their job is to do whatever I ask (always within ethical, moral, etc. boundaries).

---

[3] Proverbs 16:18 b

Sharing credit, giving credit to others, even above exactly what was earned, having the attitude of "What can I do for you?" is showing humility. Being able to actually help the person and having pride in their accomplishment as well as yours is what you want. Ignoring your contributions and only thinking of others will eventually lead to resentment, pain, and a reduction in your ability to accomplish more difficult tasks. If you cannot communicate where you have been, why should someone help you advance?

Writing a resume is an exercise where you MUST identify, quantify, and communicate your accomplishments. If you are uncomfortable acknowledging your accomplishments, you will have a hard time filling out your resume and then interviewing.

Unfortunately, many people fall under one of two traps: either not documenting their accomplishments well enough, or appearing to take too much credit for accomplishments. In reality, an accomplishment can often be taken either way, depending on the person making it and the person hearing or reading it. Chapters later in this book will help you document your accomplishments. You will be responsible for ensuring the accuracy and credit you take in the accomplishments.

Job

If you are told to do something illegal or unethical, will you do it? While this may seem like an extreme question, people face it all the time. Usually, if you say "No," you risk losing your job. Is your job that important to you? Something else to think about in that circumstance: is if it comes out that you did do something illegal or unethical, even at risk of losing your job, you could lose your career, your family, and even your freedom. Is it worth it? Outsiders will always say NO! It is never worth it. When you are the one putting your job on the line, you have a decision to make: Yes or No.

Some people will never have to make such an extreme ethical or moral decision at work. Sometimes it is a decision as to whether or not to take a job, whether or not to go on a business trip, whether to work a certain distance from home or what hours to work. I know several people who have chosen jobs that take them from home for several days a week, or several weeks at a time. They and their families have made the decision to do so for their own reasons. This is why identifying where your job fits into your priority list is so important. It is also why only you can set your priorities.

Career

You may feel that a priority of a job and a priority of a career are the same. My argument is that they are not.

Take a career in Information Technology (IT). Typically, a career in IT starts with a job on a helpdesk then fixing bugs in programs. This will advance to writing small programs then larger programs. Some people finish their careers at this level; others will advance to designing small programs which others will write. After graduating to designing larger programs, they may advance to a position like IT Manager. This position oversees programmers, designers, and often hardware people. There are several additional levels available for a career in IT. However my point is this: At each stop along the way, the person with a career in IT has a job related to that career.

What does it mean to have a priority of a career verses a priority of a job. If your priority is your career over a particular job, you will temper your answer to a request by asking yourself, "Will this help my career?" Having a career as a priority over a particular job can also mean that if a job stops helping your career, you can more quickly identify the change and do something about it, like look for a new job that WILL help your career.

You may make strategic changes in jobs to further your career. I once switched companies for basically the same salary, because I felt it would be better for my career. I saw more opportunity for advancement in the new company than I thought was available in the old company.

Priority Response

No matter what your order of priorities, someone will find fault with it. That does not matter. What matters is that you are comfortable with your priority order. If you are not, you are the only one who can change it. Also remember, other people may tell you to order your priorities one way, yet their priorities appear to be different.

Remember that when someone tells you to "Do as I say, not as I do," they have one of two motives:

1. They don't want you to make the same mistakes they have made. They want to impart wisdom to you. (By the way, this is what this book is about for me. I have made mistakes that I hope others will be able to avoid.)
2. They don't really believe what they are telling you, and want you to do something they are not willing to do themselves. Basically, they are hypocrites.

Always pay attention to motives. You need to judge all advice based on the motives of the person giving it. If the motives are pure, the advice tends to be good. If the motives are not pure, be careful. While the advice may be good, often there is something in the advice that you really want to avoid.

Once you have ordered your priorities, take some time to see what you do on a given day or in a given week. Do your actions agree with your priorities? If not, do you need to change your priority order or do you need to change your actions? You are the only one that can make the change.

Should you choose to change your priorities, they will not change just by you deciding to do so. Just like an addiction, you will find that there are a lot of things in your life that have been built around the order of priorities you had chosen before. These things include how you spend your time, how you spend your money, and who you "hang out" with. Making the decision to change is only the first step toward ordering your priorities in the way you want them.

Passion

If you have ordered your priorities in the previous chapter, you now need to look at your passions.

Passion is "a strong or extravagant fondness, enthusiasm, or desire"[4]

What are you passionate about? What do you have a strong enthusiasm toward? For me, it is helping people. From my first job, working for a woman with Polio and again with the job I had while in college, I was responsible for solving problems for people. I love working on other people's issues and finding solutions. Yes, I am a Fix-It person. It drives my wife nuts to want to talk with me about something that is wrong, and I want to fix the issue. She just wants to tell me about it.

How do you Determine What Your Passion is?

Answer this question: "What gets you up in the morning?" If I know I am scheduled to help someone, I wake up before my alarm goes off.

Look at what you do every day. If you have a choice between two activities, which one do you choose? What type of activity do you always choose? What do the activities you choose have in common?

---

[4] Dictionary.com

List out the choices you had in a given day, both at work and at home. Which choice did you make and why? When you go through this list over a couple of days, you will find there are commonalities. Put together the commonalities and you have a possibility for your passion.

Why Should you Try to Follow Your Passion?

If you do something during the day that you are passionate about, you tend to sleep better at night. What can you do that will give you the peace you would like?

As you look for a job, you will be deciding to spend at least 1/3 of your week at that job. You have the choice as to what that will be. If you can find a job working with your passion, you "will never have to work a day in your life."[5] You will enjoy what you are doing and look forward to doing it again the next day.

Until you find your passion, you will always be looking for something else to do. You will always be wondering if something else would make your life more meaningful.

Remember: As you identify your passion, also identify the other activities that you enjoy doing.

---

[5] Confucius

Helping businesses is something I enjoy. Using my skills to analyze a business or convert data into information to facilitate better decision making, gives me the opportunity to help a business which in turn helps the people employed by that business. The better I am at analyzing or creating tools, the more help I can provide.

There are weekends where I spend hours on Friday night and Saturday analyzing a business or going through resumes and other documents rather than other forms of relaxing. To me, spending time like this <u>is</u> relaxing. I have found a way to work in the area of my passion.

What is your passion?

Goal setting

Children are often asked, "What do you want to do when you grow up?" They give all kinds of answers, many of which we deem to be silly. It is sad that when we ask a child what their goals are, we find their responses silly.

I want to ask you:

What do you want to do when you grow up?

While you may think this is a silly question, I am serious. What do you want to do, two years from now? Five years from now? Ten years from now? Once the kids move out? In retirement? When you move to the next stage of your life?

By the way, I want the silly answers. Appropriate responses include but are not limited to:

- Climb Mount Everest
- Get Married
- Have Children
- Put kids through college
- Take a cruise to Alaska
- Become a pilot

What do you want to do _____? This is the basic question you must answer when you want to develop your goals.

Goals give you an idea what you want to do with your life. Goals also give you a focus and a definition for what you are going to be willing to do.

I have a goal of being able to give each of my children a cool vehicle when they get their drivers' licenses. To help facilitate my goal for my oldest son, I purchased a ten year-old Ford Mustang Convertible a couple of years before he turned 16. This was a way of helping to facilitate giving him a nice car that he could take care of and yet I could afford.

In the story above, you see a definition of a goal, a focus and desire to attain the goal, and steps I went through to achieve that goal.

What are your goals? Another way to look at this question is: What do you want your life to look like in two years? Five years? Ten years?

Notice the question is not, "How do you think your life will look?", rather it is "What do you WANT your life to look like?"

In order to focus your goals, let's take a look at the areas in which you need to set goals:

Faith

Family

Personal

Job

Career

Do these sound familiar? They should. They are the same areas where you had to set priorities earlier in this book.

How do you set goals in each of these areas?

Faith

Faith goals can be a little intimidating as a starting point; however, if faith is your first priority, you will have a hard time keeping it as your priority if you cannot state goals related to faith.

These goals include several different aspects of your life:

- Church
    - Position in the church
        - Member
        - Elder
        - Deacon
        - Pastor
        - Administrator
    - Role in the church
        - Teacher (Sunday School)

- Head of a ministry
  - Starting a ministry
  - Joining a ministry
- Creation
  - Living closer to nature
  - Making your life more environmentally conscious
  - Places to take vacations
  - Teaching others about _____
- Volunteering
  - Start a volunteer organization
  - Join a volunteer organization
  - Volunteer at _____

As you can see, there are many areas where you can setup your goals related to faith. What are your faith related goals?

Family

If you have children at home, some of your family goals may seem easier to set. These can include:

- Teaching son or daughter to drive
- Having son or daughter get into college (maybe even a specific college)
- Taking family trips together (where?, doing what?)
- Helping your child through school (finances, studying for exams)
- Helping your child purchase a house

If you do not have children, your goal may be to have children.

Family goals also include getting married, having your kids get married, participating in family activities, and setting specific goals related to your spouse.

Where do want to you see your family in two years?

- What will it look like?
- How many people in your family?
- Where will you live?
- What kind of living space will you be in?

Answer these same questions about your family in five years and ten years. What do you want your family be like?

Personal

Personal goals can include anything specifically related to you. These goals can deal with what kind of car you want to drive, skills you want to develop, or things that you want to accomplish. Personal goals are about you.

When you were setting priorities and considering "yourself" as a priority, what did you see that you needed to work on? Did you need to lose or gain weight? Stop doing something (smoking, drinking) or start doing something (going to the gym, taking a class)?

These are the components that make up your personal goals.

Again ask yourself, where do you want to see yourself in two years? Five years? Ten years?

What do you want to be doing?

Career
Considering where you are now, what do you want to see your career looking like in two years? Five years? Ten years?

You should also ask yourself if the career you have now is the same one you want to have in the future. If you see yourself changing careers, this is a great way to identify what you would like to do.

For instance, if you are looking at retiring in ten years, what do you intend retirement to look like?

Following your Goals
Just because you have made goals does not mean they will come true. In fact, setting your goals is only the first step in making them come true. The second is to plan how to get from where you are now to your goals. You may find that there is no way of attaining your goal in the time you have allotted. For instance, if you intend to retire by age 55 and you are 50 now, you had better have a lot of savings, or define retirement as doing work you will be paid for.

What do you need to do to get from where you are now to where you want to be? If you want to be CEO of a company in five years, you need to map out a plan as to how to get there. Your plan might include finding a job with an organization where you can develop the skills you will need as CEO. Identifying the type of company and positions within those companies that will help you attain your goal is very important.

When you have a map of where you are going and steps to follow to get where you want to go, you will then have a guide to help you decide what to do in certain situations.

Remember, you may wind up changing your goals on a specific level; however, it is impossible to change something that does not exist. Making changes to a goal is much better than aimlessly taking whatever you can in the hope that everything will work out fine in the end.

Identifying Desired Job

What do you want to do? What are you good at?

I believe that EVERYONE has skills that are needed somewhere. When in their proper element, EVERYONE has the potential to be a star. Outside their element, EVERYONE has the potential to fail.

When trying to identify your desired job, you have two options:

1. Try to think up every possibility and pick one.
2. Systematically look at your history and determine what you liked, did not like, were skilled at, what you failed at, and what you felt the most comfortable doing.

My recommendation is the second. Trying to think up every possibility for what you would like to do is an exercise in futility. Later in this chapter, you will find questionnaires to help you identify your desired job, but first:

Why should you use a system to identify your desired job? To answer this, let's take a look at what I am defining "Desired Job" to be.

Your desired job consists of the next work environment for you, in which you will be able to develop your skills and fulfill your passions. For each person this can be different. If you have determined your passion to be working on cars, a job that allows you to work on cars would be great; however, a job that allows you the time and ability to work on cars may also work. For instance, working as a mechanic might be a good choice; however, working at a job where you have access to the parts you need and the time to work on your own car (because you get out of work at a time so it is possible) may be even better.

Your choice for your desired job relates to:

- Your skills. The skills you have now will help you determine what job you can do. Each job should also stretch your skills and teach you new skills. Using the example of a mechanic, if you have never changed the oil in your car, you probably should not be looking for a job as a mechanic. If you feel you still want to be a mechanic, you should develop your skills and experience in this area before you start looking for a job. There are many technical schools that will help you develop the knowledge and skills to help you get started. That is what they are there for.

- The size of company or organization. Some people thrive in large companies. Some people would rather work for small companies. The difference between the two can be the

difference between being happy in your job and being miserable.
- The ownership of the company. Do you like working directly for the owner of a company or do you prefer to work in a company with several layers of management? Some people prefer to know exactly what is going on in a company; others want someone else to tell them what is going on. The more layers of management, the more opportunities for advancement. It is really hard to move up in an organization if the only position above you is the owner.
- Your passion. As stated earlier, you can make a decision to follow your passion in your workplace, or your workplace can allow you the opportunity to pursue your passion. The decision is yours and is best made after you have determined what your passion is.

Without a system, it will be extremely difficult to identify and keep track of all of these criteria. Parts of the system I am presenting here I first found in several books by the 5 O'clock Club[6]. Their methodology is an excellent resource for developing resumes.

---

[6] "Shortcut your Job Search" (Five O'Clock Club) and other Five O'Clock Club Books

The system is:

1. Tell multiple stories about jobs or events you were a part of. These stories can be good or bad. Write them down. This will help you see what is important to you.
2. Go through the stories looking for themes. These themes can be good or bad. You may find that only one story has a particular theme that is important to you.
3. Write down the themes. This allows you to document your thoughts, and, therefore, develop the criteria for your desired job.
4. If you feel something is missing, repeat the above steps as many times as you feel necessary.
5. Investigate what industries, jobs, companies, etc. are consistent with the themes you found in your stories.
6. Develop your main resume around the positive themes you found.
7. Before you interview, re-read the stories of your successes. Having these written down allows you to remember good experiences and boost your emotions just before going into an interview.
    a. Re-reading the stories also provides you answers to questions about how you

handled situations, that get asked in the interview.

The next several pages are questionnaires designed to help you understand yourself better. Filling out these questionnaires and writing down the complete stories as requested will help you determine your skills, what you like and dislike, and what you find fulfillment in. For each person, the answers will be different. Take your time with the rest of this chapter and use several separate sheets of paper to answer the questions. The more time you spend, the more accurate you will be in determining your desired job.

Job History – Tell me a story

In this section, for each of the companies, answer the following questions:

1. What did you do to help the company?
2. Did you devise a process to save money for the company?
3. Did you improve a process that helped the effectiveness of the company?
4. How can you save the new company money by using your same skill set?

Company last worked for:

Job Description and Job Accomplishments:

Stories from the job:

Name of story:

Story:

Other Company worked for:

Job Description:

Stories from the job:

Name of story:

Story:

Projects worked on
Company:

Project:

Description of Project:

What role did you play:

Company:

Project:

Description of Project:

What role did you play:

Company:

Project:

Description of Project:

What role did you play:

Interests

After reviewing the above stories, answer the following questions:

What are the common themes from more than one story above?

What do you like to do?

What kind of organization do you most like to be a part of? (Size, Ownership/Leadership Style [Family Owned/Operated, Hierarchy, Flat, Relaxed, Strict], etc.)

What do you find fulfillment in?

Do you prefer learning or teaching? Why?

What would the perfect job look like?

Identify Weaknesses/Areas for Growth

In this section, fill out multiple copies of this questionnaire, one for each job/experience that you can think of. This is about identifying what could cause you not to succeed in a new position. If you know what you need to avoid, sometimes it can help you identify what will work best for you. This section also shows what you need to work on. For instance, if you are uncomfortable around people or around computers, this may be something you look to avoid and also something you work on in your personal life. Most jobs today involve interaction with people as well as interaction with computers.

Describe a bad or uncomfortable job experience:

Company: Dates:
What happened?

How did you and your co-workers handle the situation?

What could have been done better/differently?

What did you learn?

What does this experience demonstrate that you should avoid?

What does this experience demonstrate you need to work on?

Summary

What are you afraid of?

List all of the Areas for Growth from previous questions:

What should you avoid in your job search?

How can you improve in your areas for growth?

Become an Expert

With technology advancements moving quickly, there is always a need for experts; someone who thoroughly understands a subject and is willing to share that understanding.

If you do not have a job, you have an opportunity that employed people do not have. You can spend the time necessary to become an expert on a subject. While this chapter will focus on writing articles and public speaking, if you become an expert on a subject you are passionate about, when the time comes for writing your resume and interviewing, you will have developed knowledge and skills in the area of your passion. This will help you in writing your resume as well as interviewing.

A friend of mine was laid-off. He had been an editor for a newspaper when they decided to downsize. He and I spoke about what he was looking to do next. Several people had suggested that he start an online newspaper. His concern was that he didn't know what to write about. My suggestion for him was that he become an expert. Topics I suggested included:

- Why are newspapers failing throughout the United States? What can be done about it?

- Why is the United States losing jobs? What can be done to change this trend?

- What does the United States offer that other countries do not? Basically, what do we export? What can we do to develop jobs in the United States rather than overseas?

While these topics were not in his specialty, they are topics that he could turn into a business or use to get his foot in the door for an interview.

How does this work? How can you become a recognized expert? Remember, to be perceived as an expert, you need to build credibility in your topic.

1. Pick your topic. Don't be too broad, nor too narrow. As you research your topic, you will find topics that complement yours, it is important to understand a lot about those topics as well. An example would be Computer Security. This topic is too broad. Narrow it down to something like Social Media Security Risks. The related topics you should know about then would include Viruses, Trojan Horses, Malware, Spyware, VPN's, and securing web sites.
2. Research your topic. How does your topic affect people? What problems exist? How can these problems be solved? What future

problems may arise? How can these problems be avoided? What will need to be done to solve these problems in the future? Research is never complete. Keep on researching to find new problems and innovative ways to solve them.

3. Write articles about your topic. Put your thoughts together and let someone else read them. Find people to critique your work and let you know when you are making a mistake. Finding those people who will not just tell you "Great Job" every time you give them something, is a treasure.

4. Create a blog about your topic. Blogs can be free. Publishing relevant articles about your topic will begin the process of giving you credibility. Make sure you tie the blog to an e-mail account (also can be obtained for free) so your readers can respond to you. Publish articles at least once a week, but typically no more often than once a day. Publishing too often will cause gaps once you run out of material you have already written, but not publishing often enough will cause people to forget about you between posts.

5. Read and comment on other related blogs. When writing your articles, be sure to read other blogs and comment on them. The more relevant the comments, the more likely people

will follow your links back to your blog and provide relevant comments. This will also increase your credibility.
6. Create a social media presence. This step will change over time, however at the time of this writing, creating a Twitter account, and Facebook Fan Pages are the minimum you need to do. These allow for further distribution of your ideas, increasing your credibility and helping others to understand your ideas.

To turn being an expert into income, you need to look at the following choices.

- Become a public speaker on the topic. In your research, you should have found other experts. Where do they speak? There are professional speaking organizations you can join that will help you find speaking engagements. You may not be able to charge at first, however if you are a good speaker with an engaging topic, you will develop a base and be able to charge for your knowledge.
- Become a consultant. If you have experience in the area in which you become an expert, look around. Is there a way you could consult for companies that need this expertise? Find the people in the organization who most need access to your expertise and begin networking with them. If they consider you an expert, they

will consult with you regarding their needs. At this time, you can further refine your research. Many people have turned consulting into a full-time job. Consulting can also be done on a part-time basis once you land a job. This is an excellent source of additional income.

- Become a teacher. Do you have expertise in an area in which you could train people? Identify the potential clients and determine whether or not they or their companies would be willing to pay for classes in your topic. For instance, if you are an expert on Microsoft Excel, setting up training classes where you present your knowledge for a few hours once or twice a week, can help you break into consulting as well as provide income from teaching. Remember teaching does not always have to be on-site or in a classroom. With the tools that are now available (WebEx, WebConference.com, etc.) you can teach people across the world, from the comfort of your home.

- Write a book. You can mix-n-match the above options. This one you should do in conjunction with one or more of the other options. Writing a book means that you have spent time to develop your thoughts and have someone critically review them. A published author has much more credibility than someone that just stands in front of people and pontificates on a subject. Most of the seminar speakers you have heard probably state that they have a book available for purchase. This provides additional income for the speaker (maybe the only income from that event) as well as residual information to the reader. Books do not have to be published by a major publisher to have an effect on readers. There are many ways you can self publish or work with a publishing company that specializes in small orders.

- Develop a web site. If you want to earn money from your expertise, **you must develop a web site**. This is where you can completely control the interaction with those who are looking at your work. Providing additional, timely information to people will keep them coming back and allow you to sell books, provide classes, reference other experts' materials, and is seen as the minimum requirement of an expert.

Please understand that this is not meant to be the final word on becoming an expert on a topic. This is meant to give you an overview and allow you to see if it is right for you.

Becoming an expert can help advance your career due to your advanced knowledge. Companies like to hire an expert in a field. This provides a comfort level, that the expert will know what to do, better than someone who is not an expert.

Volunteering

I often see resumes of people who were laid-off for several months to years. Other resumes have large gaps between jobs. The perception most of these resumes give is that the person is lazy or at least has not done anything productive since the last time they had a job. Statistics show that it is easier for someone who has a job to be hired, than for someone who is unemployed. The reason is because of that perception. How do you get around this perception? One way is volunteering.

Why should you volunteer?

The right kind of volunteering accomplishes the following:

- Helps you give back to your community
- Helps you identify and develop your passion
- Enhances your skills
- Teaches you new skills
- Keeps you busy
- Gets you out of the house
- Shows a positive side of your personality
- Puts you together with people who care about the same things you care about
- Lets you try out a new field
- Looks good on a resume
- Removes gaps in a resume

Volunteering falls under two categories. Working for a volunteer organization and performing organized volunteer work.

Working for a Volunteer Organization

Many volunteer organizations hire paid personnel. As you look for a job, if you are volunteering for an organization that also has employees, you may have the opportunity to be hired. Most of these organizations want to hire people that show they are interested in the interests of the organization. When you volunteer, you show interest. You also show how hard a worker you are and how well you would work out in the organization.

Being hired by a volunteer organization that focuses on your passion can help you have more than just a job, you can fulfill your passion and earn a living at the same time.

Performing Organized Volunteer Work

What does it mean to perform organized volunteer work? Is showing up early or staying late at church in order to help clean up, volunteer work? Yes, however it is not Organized Volunteer Work.

Organized Volunteer Work is when you put your time into something specific on a regular basis. This can be handling the phones for a telethon, to every week delivering flowers and reading at a retirement home, to organizing volunteers to clean parks on weekends. Doing something organized on a regular basis is a great way to get you out of the house. Volunteering will also give you something you are interested in to talk about in an interview or when you are in a group of people. Why does this matter? The last time you were in a group of people and someone asked "What's New?" what did you answer? "Nothing", "Not Much", or . . .

"I am volunteering in an organization that cleans parks on Saturdays. Last Saturday, I was at _____ Park with about 100 other volunteers. It was an amazing day, outside cleaning up all of the trash. I could not believe how many bags of trash we collected. I would never have thought that a park could be such a mess. . . ."

Which response sounds better? Personally, I would rather talk about picking up trash in a park than that I sent out 10 more resumes. I would also rather listen to a story about picking up trash than hearing "Nothing".

In order to understand where you fit in volunteering, fill out the questionnaire below. This is designed to help you think about what you are interested in and what skills you have. When you have completed this questionnaire, take a look around you and see if there is some place you can volunteer that will feed your interests or better yet, your passion. If not, what about organizations that can help you get off the couch, out of the house, and give back to your community?

If there are no volunteer organizations you could join, start one. Organize cleaning the park, go to hospitals or retirement communities and volunteer. There are things that everyone can do. If you cannot read out loud (I personally HATE reading out loud) tell stories. The key is to get out and get involved.

Giving Back to Your Community

There are many people in your community that are helping you whether you know it or not. These people have volunteered their time, chosen careers and dedicated their resources to see that you and other people have the opportunity to succeed. If you don't believe me, take a look at some of the people around you that could be working at other jobs, yet are doing what they believe in, in order to see other people are safe and succeed. For instance, pastors and other church staff, teachers, trash collectors, firemen, police officers, etc. These people could be working at other jobs, often making more money than they are at their current positions, and yet they choose to help other people. They deserve our thanks.

Your choice to give back to your community will help you as well. Doing work for other people is a great way to get your attitude right. After all, no-one wants to be around, let alone hire, someone who has a bad attitude or acts like the world revolves around them. Attitude makes a major difference between looking for a job and keeping a job. It is hard to hide a bad attitude, however someone who is willingly helping out others usually has a good attitude that other people enjoy being around.

The next few pages contain a questionnaire to help you determine where you should investigate volunteering. Some people have a hard time narrowing down the opportunities; others need help figuring out if there is an opportunity for them. Fill out the following questionnaire as completely as you can. When you review your answers, you will have a better glimpse of what opportunities will work best for you.

Volunteering Questionnaire

What do you enjoy:

    Teaching – What, who, setting

    Cleaning

    Cooking

    Reading Aloud

    Flower Arranging

    Gardening

    Sports – Playing, Organizing, Coaching

    Organizing

    Child Care

    Playing an instrument

    Singing

    Research – What Type

    Writing

    Designing printed materials

    Developing Web Materials

    Social Media

Other _____

What are you good at?

What are your Vocational/Job Related Skills?

What skills do you utilize in your personal life?

What family members live close to you? What are they involved in?

If you have children, what are they involved in?

What volunteer opportunities are around you?

What would you want to do as volunteer work?

Education – Benefits vs. Expectations

Each of us has gone through some level of education. Whether we received a PHD or never graduated from high school, we had some education. There are many types of education, and which level you need, or should pursue, depends on the type of job you desire. Also, typically, the higher the degree, the better you will be paid.

Education, whether it results in a degree or certification, demonstrates a person's willingness to accept a task and complete it. Most education teaches you how to think and where to find answers to questions. While you memorize facts, the facts become useful as you put them together in different ways in order to solve an issue or answer a question.

When I was in college, several of my professors had degrees in subjects other than what I was studying. Did that make them less of a professor? No. They were able to put together information in a different way to make the lessons meaningful, no matter what specific area you were studying. A college education really shows that you have an understanding of several topics and are able to look for answers to questions.

I have found that many of the classes I took while in school have benefitted me, even though I did not enjoy the class at the time. For instance, I have had several classes in English. Since I am writing this book, apparently it made a difference in my life and hopefully many other people who will read this book.

I also spent a lot of time studying math. In math, specifically, Geometry, there is a concept of proofs. I HATED working on proofs. When my oldest son got into Geometry, I was reminded again how much I hated proofs. HOWEVER, when I was going through proofs with my son, I realized I used proofs EVERY DAY. Not the kinds of postulates and theorems that are used in Geometry, but each day I was basically providing a proof to someone that would show them how something I was working on was true or correct. As I "Show my Work," which I was told to do many times by my teachers, I learned that when I do that now, the person reading my work can go back through, find any mistakes I made, and become much more comfortable with the solution I have provided. People around me that do not show their work, often find they are being questioned, and their results not believed, simply because the person reading the results does not understand how they arrived at their results.

This is a long way of saying that an education is very important. Even taking classes that are not of immediate interest to you, allows you to expand you knowledge and understanding of the world around you, which in turn helps you relate to the people around you.

Specialized Education

When you leave school and want to start in your career, you have a choice to make. What additional schooling do you need? Most careers offer certifications. For instance, in Computers, there are certifications that range from Cisco Certified Engineer to MCSE to A+ to . . . There are certifications for teaching certain classes, certifications for erecting scaffold, you may also have an apprenticeship program you must complete to become a master at your chosen craft. Each of these certifications or apprenticeship programs is additional education. While they might not give you a degree, they will require concentrated study and preparation in order to pass the tests to obtain that certification.

Is it worth obtaining specialized education if you are out of a job?

Usually. Most of the time, any education or training, even if it is not directly within your field, is a great thing to do. If you teach Math, for instance, taking computer courses may enable you to integrate between the two or even teach another type of class. Any learning is productive.

The No part of "Is it worth obtaining a specialized education?" falls into the categories of: Does the cost outweigh the benefit? and Will this training get you a job that you want and are willing to do?

I have talked with several people who took out student loans to learn new skills and over a year after they graduated, they still did not have a job in their field. If the training helped them get a better job than they had, it was probably good, if they are simply adding to their monthly expenses in order to pay off student loans, and they have not found a position that will help them make the money they need, the argument can be made that taking the additional classes was a waste of money.

Online Classes

In 2009, I started hearing about free online classes. Some of these classes were put online by reputable learning institutions and allows someone to view a lecture or presentation and not have to pay for the class. I love this idea. Being able to take classes in the area I am interested in, without having to spend the money or time to physically go back to school is a great idea.

HOWEVER there is a caution about documenting your free online classes. At this point, most people do not associate the free classes with the quality you would receive from a more formal education. This is changing, but right now, putting down on a resume that you completed a free online class is typically viewed as you brushing up on your skills. If you have no other experience or education in the area of the class, most people are discounting you taking the class.

In the future, free online classes will probably be documented better and therefore be a good way to show on a resume that you are continuing to learn new skills; however, the future is not here yet.

Finances

After I graduated from college, and was hired for my first job, I did what most people do. I went out and bought a brand new car. My justification was that I needed a new car since the one I had been driving was old and would probably break down soon. What I failed to do was get rid of the old car. We made this decision so my wife would also have a car. So with a new income, we wound up adding a car payment to our monthly expenses as well as adding a car to our insurance and having to put fuel into both vehicles.

Unfortunately, this is what happens to a lot of people. They get a job, then go out and get a new car, move to a new apartment, buy a house, or make some other major change to their monthly costs, without taking into consideration what this will mean under their new income. Another common mistake people make is to forget about the taxes that they will be paying. That monthly income of $2,000, can drop below $1,500 simply by having to pay taxes. Subtract from this any money that you intend to put into retirement or health insurance, and the take-home money you can use to pay your bills continues to drop.

Many people assume when they get a job that it will solve their financial problems. This is not always true. Identifying your financial needs before applying for jobs can reduce the chances of getting into a job that will not meet your needs. Also remember, just because you need a certain amount per month does not mean you will find a position that will pay you that much.

There are several costs that can occur once you land a job. These costs include:

- Childcare – if you are not working, you probably are not paying for your kids to be in child care. Once you begin working, the decision will need to be made as to what to do.
- Additional travel expenses (fuel, bus or train fare, parking, vehicle maintenance) – You currently have some travel expenses, however if you will be traveling ½ an hour a day to and from work, that will increase your fuel expenses as well as the vehicle maintenance expenses. Will you have to pay for parking at work? If you are working in a city, that is a possibility.
- Clothing – some jobs require uniforms. If you will have to purchase a uniform, it will create additional costs for you. Even if you do not have a uniform, most jobs do not allow you to just come in to work in jeans and a t-shirt. The nicer clothing costs more and therefore will add additional expenses.
- Equipment – does your new employer make you purchase your own equipment? If you are in construction, you may have to bring and

maintain your own hand tools. Tools break and have to be replaced, adding costs, often when you can least afford them.
- Meals – purchasing lunch every day is a lot more expensive than eating at home. Will you be eating out at night more often because you do not feel like cooking or waiting until food is done?

When you are looking for a job it is also a good time to review your monthly budget and cut back where you can. This will enable you to be more flexible when applying for the positions that will work out best for you.

One of the most disheartening experiences is getting excited about a new job just to find out that your take-home pay every month is not enough to cover your needs. Avoiding this disappointment will help you have a better attitude and be better able to focus on being the best employee you can be.

The following chart is a worksheet to help you identify where you currently stand with regard to your finances. You may find that you are "under water" now. Work with this worksheet to develop a budget you can live with now and again when you land a job. Also, use this worksheet to determine what your monthly income needs to be. It is always better to know before you accept a job, rather than after.

Job Cost Worksheet

In this worksheet you will find categories to break apart your monthly expenses. Please add any additional categories you need in order to get a good perspective on what your monthly financial needs are. Remember, if you do not pack a lunch each day, you will probably be purchasing lunch which typically runs between $5.00 and $10.00 a day. At 22 days a month, lunches can run $220 a month on top of your grocery budget. Taking a lunch of leftovers or a sandwich can cut the cost to about $2.00 a day or $44 a month.

Monthly Expenses

	Current Costs	Additional with Job	Total Cost
Rent/Mortgage			
Moving Expenses			
Insurance			
Groceries			
Lunches			
Morning Coffee			
Fast Food			
Restaurants			
Clothing			
Job Related Clothing			
Laundry			
Child Care			
School expenses			
Vehicle			

Fuel			
Public Transportation			
Insurance			
Entertainment			
Movies			
Restaurants			
Cable TV			
Internet			
Utilities			
Gas			
Electric			
Phone			
Cell Phone			
Health Insurance			
Outstanding Bills			
Loan Repayment			

Social Media

"Everyone is doing it." "No one will know." "My friends made me do it."

Even when you were a kid, those lines didn't work. I remember my mom saying many times, "If everyone jumped off a bridge, would you?" Unfortunately, people don't seem to remember this advice when it comes to social media. There are times (many times) when, even when your friends are doing something, you should not. For instance, if you went to an awesome party over the weekend, posting pictures is not usually a wise idea.

When you are looking for a job, many companies will search social media to see what they can find out about a candidate.

Have you ever Googled yourself? Try it sometime. You will often find postings from your Facebook page, Twitter account, MySpace account, and sometimes pictures from those pages. If someone does not know you and this is what they see, would the information they find by searching your name on a search engine make them want to hire you? What about once you have a job? Will they want to keep you? Would they want to give you a promotion?

There are ways that social media can help you. If you are becoming an expert on a topic, a good way to interact with people is through social media. If you read the previous chapter on becoming an expert, you will see that social media is specifically recommended at times.

The news is full of stories where social media hurt a career. Some companies do not allow their employees to be on social media. Other companies monitor their employees' social media accounts to ensure they do not represent the company badly.

I heard a story about a woman who was being fired from her job. While in the exit interview, she was on her phone updating her Facebook status, even while Human Resources was talking to her. While this is extremely rude, is she thinking about how it will affect her next job search? If a future employer saw that she was updating her status while being fired, they may not get the impression of her maturity that she would want them to have.

Other stories include people who have "Friended" their boss and later updated their status that they were at an event, when they had called in sick to work. Others have posted pictures on their pages of themselves in compromising positions or situations (drunk, etc), or said things about their boss, without paying attention to whom they have "Friended". If you are looking to start a company and you are friends with or linked to your boss, be careful what you say. If they read your information at all, you may be giving your notice to them, without realizing it.

The moral of this story is: If you choose to use social media, be careful. Make sure you do not say anything about anyone that you would not say in-front of them. Also, be VERY careful as to who you are friends with. While it may be cool to have 1,000,000 friends, someone posting the wrong thing to your account can get you fired or may cause you to lose a potential job.

Your mother told you to pick your friends wisely – that is STILL good advice.

If you are a professional, LinkedIn is one social network you may want to join. One advantage to LinkedIn is the concept of recommendations. You can recommend other people and have them recommend you. The caution with LinkedIn is just like any other social media network. If you are connected to your boss, or anyone else that you would rather not know about your job search, be careful where you say you work and what you are looking for.

Self employment

When a person loses a job, they often think about starting their own business, "Being their own Boss." This can be a good time to try something new; however, you MUST be aware of the risks and even dangers in order to make a wise decision.

There are many ways to be in business part-time as well as full-time. For an entrepreneur, part-time often equates to 40 to 50 hours a week, full-time requires additional time. I realize you are probably thinking I am lying, however once you get started, if you are working in the area of your passions, and if you want to earn money for what you are doing, you will find that it takes a lot of time.

Multi-Level Marketing

For all the bad things people say about multi-level marketing, it is a way you can get into your own business part time, and many people have become successful. Multi-level marketing can help you learn your strengths and weaknesses. Multi-level marketing organizations also have training classes and can help someone who is very interested in their products. The issues with most multi-level marketing companies are the initial cost before there is any income, and selling to your friends. If you are uncomfortable selling to your friends, it can be hard to develop your business in a multi-level marketing organization.

Become an expert

There is a whole chapter on becoming an expert. In that chapter there are a list of ways you can make money as an expert including consulting, writing a book, and speaking engagements. If you are not employed, this can be a way of boosting your knowledge in your field and getting some income at the same time.

Mistakes/Risks

If and when you start thinking about going into business for yourself you need to do a couple of things:

1. Consult your Spouse – If you have a spouse, make sure they are on-board with your decision
2. Consult your Accountant – You are making major money decisions where you will need to understand how the decisions affect your taxes, financial planning, retirement, etc. Your accountant is absolutely necessary to keep you from having a lot of trouble in the future.
3. Consult your Attorney – What kind of business organization should you have? What are the laws associated with the business you are looking at? What other risks that you have not identified do you need to be aware of? Your attorney is the one that can help you stay out of

trouble and make you aware of some of the consequences of your decisions.
4. Find a Business Mentor – Find someone that understands business, whether or not they are in the same business you want to start. This person can help you with the practical aspects of what you are going through. They can help you make decisions that you do not even know exist.

Areas where you are likely to make mistakes or will have risks that you may be unaware of include:

- Taxes
    - Business
    - Payroll
    - Property
- Business Licenses
- Incorporating your Business
    - DBA
    - Sole Proprietorship
    - Partnership
    - LLC/LLP
    - S Corp
    - C Corp
- Insurance
    - Business
    - Errors and Omissions
    - Health
    - Liability

- - Workers Comp
- Hiring Personnel
- Invoicing/Cash Flow
- Paying Bills
- Training yourself, personnel, customers, etc.
- Researching products and services

Applications

When you go to an interview, most companies have you fill out an application, even if you have already submitted a resume. The application fulfills several requirements for the company.

1. Standardizing the application process
2. Ensuring all necessary information is provided

Since you will need to fill out an application, having an application already filled out, so you can simply copy the information onto the company's specific form, will allow you to quickly and accurately fill out the necessary information. Thus you will be able to demonstrate that you are organized, prepared, and ready to fulfill their needs. If you do not have a sample application filled out, you may have to try to come up with the information off the top of your head, thus you run the risk of inaccuracy as well as appearing to not be ready for the interview.

Standardizing the Application Process

When a company is doing interviews and they have several candidates for a position, they need a standardized way to evaluate candidates. What a candidate fills out on an application is the first of those ways. Another way is with the questions that are asked.

In the Interview chapter, we will cover questions asked of a candidate.

Why would a company want to have a standardized application process? Standardized forms eliminate much of the variables associated with reviewing a person's qualifications. If you fill out an application, it does not matter if your resume is 1 page or 3 pages. It also does not matter what size font you use, nor any of the myriad of decisions associated with how your resume appears. Some companies that have you fill out an application online will go as far as having a computer program go through their applications and rate each application based on how well the candidate meets the requirements of the position. This is often handled by a program going through the application looking for the key words associated with the position to see if they are used, and ranking an application based on the number of key words used.

Don't worry about whether or not this is fair, it is what happens. Frankly, if a company has 30 applications to go through for a single position, they need some way to identify who the best candidates are.

If you know this, you can improve your chances by correctly using the key words that are associated with the position you are applying for. If you see an advertisement for the position, make sure you use as many of the key words from that advertisement as you reasonably can, in your application.

Ensuring all Necessary Information is Provided

Having seen many resumes, I have seen where it appeared someone had large gaps in their employment. What had actually happened was that they had worked for companies outside the area for which they were applying. If I were to only look at the resume, I would have missed the most recent jobs they have had. Applications eliminate this issue. They request the last 3 to 5 jobs the candidate has had. This way, even if it is unrelated, the employer is better able to judge a person's work experience.

When you go to an interview or even when you apply for a position, you will have to fill out an application. Answering the following questions will help you have a single document that will enable you to quickly and accurately complete the application.

Sample Application

Name:

Present Address:

How long have you lived at this address?

Social Security Number:

Telephone Number:

Education

	Name	Location	No. years Completed	Major/ degree
High School				
College				
Bus or Trade School				
Other Education				

Have you ever been convicted of a crime?   If Yes, explain:

Have you ever been bonded?   If Yes, when and are you still bonded?

Do you have any clearances? If so, which?

Drivers License Number

Drivers License State

Expiration Date

Do you have any special licenses? If so, which and when do they expire?

Have you ever been in the armed forces?   If so, Discharge Date:

Job Experience
List your last 3 employers

1. Name of Company
   Address
   Phone Number
   Title/Job Description
   Supervisor
   Employment Dates
   Reason for Leaving
2. Name of Company

       Address
       Phone Number
       Title/Job Description
       Supervisor
       Employment Dates
       Reason for Leaving
3. Name of Company
       Address
       Phone Number
       Title/Job Description
       Supervisor
       Employment Dates
       Reason for Leaving

References

Other than relatives, list 4 references:

Name:

Relation to you:

Telephone number:

Name:

Relation to you:

Telephone number:

Name:

Relation to you:

Telephone number:

Name:

Relation to you:

Telephone number:

Special Skills or Accomplishments

Resume

We are finally getting to the topic for which you probably picked up this book. Your Resume. How do you write it? What does the perfect resume look like?

Unfortunately, as you have seen in previous chapters, this chapter will not be an exhaustive dissertation on resumes. There are many books on how to write a resume. Instead, we will focus on:

- What should your resume say?
- What should be in a resume?
- What should not be in a resume?
- Changing What to So What

Something to keep in mind: When you send a resume in to apply for a job, you are probably competing against 50 to 100 other people for 1 position. You will have about 30 seconds to make your first impression. Many resumes will get less time than that. If you cannot impress within 30 seconds, you will probably not get the job. You may lengthen the time someone will take with your resume by having more than 1 page.

You will spend a lot of time developing your resume and hopefully spend a lot of time preparing a cover letter and sending all of this information to a prospective employer. If you don't give them a reason to look further, they do not have the time to read and understand your resume.

Your resume is a single document where you are trying to convince someone to interview you. Anything else you try to do in your resume will detract from its one and only purpose. In order to convince someone to interview you, you must answer two questions. These questions are:

- What am I looking to do?
- What will I do for your company?

What am I Looking to Do?

I speak with many people who are looking for a job. The first question I ask is, "What kind of job are you looking for?" The response I usually get is, "Anything." Hopefully, you know what you want to do since you have gone through the chapter Identifying your Desired Job. Now you need to tell the reader of your resume, the same thing.

Writing a Better Objective Statement

Most people use an Objective Statement. Unfortunately most objective statements are something like:

My objective is to get a job at ABC Company in the Accounts Receivable department, utilizing my skills.

Unfortunately this objective is useless and for that reason many people leave it off their resume completely.

Having put together what your Desired Job is, take the key components of that job and put it into a statement. This will be much more meaningful and useful to the people who will be reviewing your resume. It can also give your resume focus.

Take a look at a statement like:

My objective is to utilize my analytical skills to help advance Accounts Receivable policies and procedures to increase collections and lower agings.

Such a statement will be more meaningful to the person reading it. This helps tell them exactly what you are looking for, rather than them having to guess or assume something.

What will I Do For Your Company?

Which is a better point for your resume? (By the way, the capitalization is on purpose)

1. Managed audits for the company including the annual financial audits, annual Workers Compensation audits, union audits, and an IRS audit.

2. Saved a $30,000,000 company over $1,000,000 in 12 months by managing Financial, Workers Compensation, Union and IRS Audits

Which person would you want to hire?

What you Will Do is answered by what you have done in the past. This is turning the What (point 1) into the So What (point 2). One way to show what you Will Do is to Quantify what you have done. Put numbers to the bullet points. How much have you saved? How many have you saved, made, etc? These numbers must be real. They can be in terms of dollars, items, time, or whatever is most meaningful. Remember, saving 1 hour a week equates to 52 hours a year or almost a week and a half a year. This is significant savings to a company.

A resume is your opportunity to impress someone, when you have thought out every part of the document ahead of time. Show this in your resume by doing the following:

- Spell-check your resume – I have seen many resumes which have obvious spelling mistakes. Since you should be typing your final resume on a computer, there is NO EXCUSE for not using a spell checker on your resume (and by the way, your cover letter). When I read a resume that has spelling mistakes, I immediately think that this is someone that does not really want the job I am offering. They are not willing to put in even the smallest effort in order to try to impress me by simply checking out the document with a spell checker which is built into any word processor program.

- Have someone (hopefully several people) critically read your resume – I have had several resumes that I could not believe anyone had reviewed before it was sent out. It only takes a couple of minutes for someone to read and comment.
- Use Whitespace – If the person you had critically read your resume has to work to get through it, the person who is looking to hire you will not spend the time.
- Use industry terms – if you are applying for a job as a computer programmer, state the names of the languages you know. If you are applying for a job in accounting, talk about debits, credits, General Ledger, basically use terms that indicate you know what you are doing within that field.
- Be careful with industry terms that may have negative meanings – for instance, if you are applying for a job as a computer programmer, putting on a resume that you know BASIC, or are an Access programmer, gives the impression that you are not up to date and probably have never programmed

professionally. Instead, saying you know Visual BASIC or .NET gives the impression you are current and are continuing to develop your skills.

- Use industry terms CORRECTLY – When you use a term, make sure you use it correctly. If the person reading your resume has any knowledge of your industry, mis-using a term gives the impression you are careless and not willing to ensure you communicate properly.
- Do Not include your References – Provide your references when asked in an interview, NOT as part of your resume. Some employers will call references off of resumes, without even speaking with the candidate. You want to be interviewed before someone starts calling your references.

What Should Your Resume Look Like?

- Readable – Too much text means not enough reading. When you see a page that has no whitespace, you don't want to read it; nor does someone that has to look at 100 pages, just like yours. Give the person a break and make your resume readable.
- Bullet Points – Bullet points should be short and to the point. If they want more information, they can ask you in an interview.

- More than 1 page – Most resumes should be 1 ½ to 2 ½ pages long. Use the second page to start a new section (for instance your list of jobs). Below, you will see an outline of different types of Resumes. In this discussion you will see that only an Education based resume is likely to be 1 page.
- Create logical sections – Breaking your resume up into logical sections will help with the readability as well as provide highlights for your reader
- Put your best information first – If someone only reads one bullet point from each section you have, it will be your first point. Make it count so they will read on.

The layout of a resume is often considered one of the hardest parts of developing a resume. Personally I disagree. For me the hardest part is identifying what to include. This is why there are so many questionnaires included in this book. Filling out the questionnaires will help you determine what you can put in. As you focus your resume, you will go from what you **can** put in to what you **should** put in the resume.

There are many different resume layouts. Which layout you choose will depend on what type of job you are looking for and what experience you have. Three layouts are outlined below. You can find books that contain many resumes, each laid out differently. Please do some research into those books so you can determine which layout is right for you.

- Education – If you are in school or just out of school and have NO relevant work experience, an Education style resume will help demonstrate your knowledge.
- Job History – If you do not have much relevant work experience and want to showcase Where you worked rather than What you did, a Job History style of resume will work well.
- Work Experience – For most people who have a work history and can document experiences, a Work Experience style works out well. This style focuses on What you did and usually better answers the question, "What will you do for me?"

Education Resumes

Education Resumes usually have the following sections:

- Objective
- Education
- Job Experience
- Other Activities

This type of resume can be as short as 1 page because there is not a lot to say. Education resumes focus on relevant areas of study, grade point averages, schools, and specific classes. The Job Experience section is only there if the person had a job while in school, and is there to show that the person worked. Typically Job Experience is discounted by the interviewer, other than to indicate that the person might know about working outside school.

Job History Resumes

Job History Resumes usually have the following sections:

- Objective
- Job Experience
- Education
- Other Activities

This type of resume tends to be 1 ½ to 2 pages long. Jobs are listed with a paragraph or several bullet points to indicate what relevant work was done while in that position. The focus of this type of resume is continuity of jobs (no gaps or this type of resume really shows it) and that the candidate was constantly moving up in their jobs. Other than a degree or specialized education, the education portion is expected but basically ignored by the interviewer. Other activities are there only to show that the person appears to have additional interests other than work. This type of resume works well if you have worked for a company that is well known, especially in your industry.

Unless you are applying for an entry level position (in which case, you probably need an application rather than a resume), be careful using companies that hire many levels of employees such as fast food franchises, grocery or department stores. The interviewer may assume that you were stocking shelves, or handling a cash register rather than working in the office.

Work Experience Resumes

Work Experience Resumes usually have the following sections:

- Objective
- Related Experience
- Areas of Expertise
- Experience or Work Experience
- Education

There are significant differences between the Work Experience resume and the other types of resumes. Notice, there is no "Other Activities" section. Other activities are included in the Experience section. This allows the candidate to show relevant experience, no matter where or when it was obtained.

The basic concept behind a Work Experience resume is that you show what you have done (the So What/What can I do for you), then show what you are good at (the Areas of Expertise section), then show where you learned or applied these skills (the Work Experience section). The Education section is to show the degrees you have and any specialized training. Often the resume is designed so the second page is the top of the Experience or Work Experience section. This effectively gives you one page to focus on What you can do for the company you are applying to work for, and then a page to tell Where you did similar work. This provides ample opportunity for whitespace, and focusing on what is important for the interviewer to know.

If you have gaps in your resume, this type of resume allows you to handle the gaps much better than the others, since the focus is on experience and expertise rather than specific jobs. In fact, some people only include Relevant Work Experience so they have a great reason for not including every job (especially if there were gaps, unrelated jobs, or short term jobs).

Which type of resume is for you is something you will have to decide. As stated above, there are many books on the subject which will offer many opinions. Go to a library or book store and you can see specific examples of these and many other types of resumes. When you choose a type of resume, make sure it portrays your experience in the way you are most comfortable.

Here are a couple of questionnaires to help you put together the parts of your resume. These questionnaires help you answer Why a company should hire you (Quantify, So What) and put together the parts of your resume from the questionnaires that you have already filled out.

Why Should a Company Hire You?

In this section, you are developing portions of your resume as well as putting together the items to review before each interview. Make sure you quantify your answers as much as possible, for instance: Saved ABC Company 1 hour a day by implementing a more efficient method of moving product in the warehouse.

What did you do to help other companies or organizations?

1. Did you devise a process to save money for the company?
2. Did you improve a process that helped the effectiveness of the company?
3. Did you save them money? Improve efficiency? Fix a problem?
4. How can you save the new company money by using your same skill set?

What lessons have you learned that will help you in a new organization?

What education have you had? How will this help in a new position?

Tell a story about something you did that improved someone else's situation:

Resume – Put Everything Together

This questionnaire is designed to put together everything you need for a resume. Take information from all of the other questionnaires you have filled out and put it together into this one document. This should be MULTIPLE pages long. Put EVERYTHING in here, since it will be easier to remove information when it comes time to type up your final resumes, rather than have to add information.

Skills/Expertise:

Key Results:

Work/Job Experience – At least the past 10 years or last 10 jobs, whichever is less
Company Name, Date of Employment, Titles, Description of Duties, Skills Used

Education Experience:

Volunteer/Other Experience:

Recognitions:

Potential References:

Your address:

Phone number:

E-Mail Address:

Positions Desired:

Job Objectives:

Cover Letters

The first item most interviewers will read from you is your cover letter. Cover letters need to be short and to the point. There are three parts to a cover letter:

- Introduction/Where you heard about the opportunity
- Experience that matches their requirements
- Conclusion/request for interview

Many people struggle with writing cover letters, so in an effort to make it easier for you to write one, let's break down the parts.

Introduction

The first paragraph for the cover letter is an introduction paragraph, identifying what position you are applying for and where you heard about the position. If you heard about the position from someone that works at the company, put their name here.

Experience that Matches Their Requirements

The second paragraph outlines which aspects of the job you are experienced in. This is where you take the key words from the job advertisement and use them to show that you are the candidate they are looking for. It is important to use the terms they use.

I placed an advertisement for a specific type of software developer. In the advertisement, I stated that the person must have experience in a specific development environment. None of the cover letters, nor any of the resumes even referenced the environment. In fact, from the responses I received, none of the people had any idea what I was talking about, nor was it worth their time to investigate and find out what I was looking for. None of the people who applied were willing to do the research necessary to indicate to me they were worth calling for an interview.

Don't make the same mistake. Highlight your qualifications that the advertisement mentioned, and any key points that will help them decide to interview you. This paragraph can be in the form of bullet points, if you are more comfortable with them.

Conclusion/Request for Interview

At the end of the letter, you need a short (one to two sentence) paragraph, reminding them what position you are applying for and letting them know you are looking forward to speaking with them soon about an interview. While everyone knows what a cover letter is, this section solidifies the request for an interview. This paragraph leaves open the possibility of you calling the person a couple of days later to make sure they received your resume and setup an interview time.

References

Choose your references wisely. This is your chance to have 3 to 4 other people tell the company you want to work for, positive information about you.

There have been times where I received a call from a company checking references for a candidate, and I had no idea who the candidate was. There was no way I could be a good reference for them.

Who should you choose to be your reference? The first rule is NEVER choose a reference that you are not completely confident will be a good reference for you. It is better to break other rules and choose people that are not typically considered good references, rather than someone who should be a good reference that winds up saying bad things about you. Your choice also depends on the type of job and the quality of your references.

- Teachers - If you are just out of school, or even in school, and have no experience outside education, having a recent teacher as a reference, especially if they are in the same field that the job is in, is an excellent idea.
- Bosses – As long as the boss has approved you using them as a reference, they are an excellent choice. The new company you will be working

for would really like to speak with your former or current boss and this provides them the opportunity to do so. If you choose not to include a boss in your list of references, some companies will wonder about it. Remember, leaders of volunteer organizations that you are a part of, are great references as well.

- Co-Workers – If you have any co-workers it is expected that you will include them as references. They can speak to your ability to interact with others at your level or slightly above or below your level throughout the organization.

- Customers and Vendors – If your position will be working with customers or vendors, including them as references can be a great benefit. This will make the company more comfortable hiring someone who will be dealing with these relationships.

- Friends – It is assumed you were friends with everyone you put down as a reference. People who are friends outside of work can be good references but usually you need to have another connection with them other than just friendship. For instance, my wife used a couple of friends she serves on a volunteer board with as references. When they were called, one of them stated that she had hired several people in her career and had never meet anyone as dedicated and trustworthy as my wife. This was probably a better reference than anyone else would have been. Remember to choose your friends carefully, especially when it comes to using them as references.

- Family – Choose family sparingly. If you have done something specific, tangible, and meaningful; it can be ok to use family. For instance, if you cared for your ailing parent and that is why you were not in the workforce for the past couple of years, having a family member who will talk about how well you did and how dedicated you were/are, will enhance your position. Almost any other relative will not add anything. The hard part is when you work for family for years. Who do you use as a reference? Be careful, the right person MIGHT do well as a reference.

If you can provide a reference from inside the company, it is usually best to do so. Inside references are always more believable for the person checking your references, than outside references. Do choose even inside references carefully. If the person you know has an abrasive personality, don't specifically use them as a reference on your reference list, mention that you know them and where you know them from. NEVER say anything bad about them; just the fact that you do not use them as a reference will be enough.

When someone provides a reference for you, you represent them.

One place I worked, I hired someone from church. This person worked out really well. Everyone was happy with his progress and performance. About 7 months after he was hired, another person from church needed a job and we had an opening. I presented this person for the position. While he was not originally the top candidate, he wound up getting the job. At the same time, I hired two other people from church to work for me. Within a year of hiring the first person, Human Resources was coming to me to ask if I knew anyone who could fill open positions. The people I provided a reference for were so good that my reputation as well as theirs kept improving.

Before the hiring process began, I had a great reputation in the company. Then, the people I hired and provided references for, represented me. When they were hired, our reputations were tied together. If they had messed up, it would have reflected badly on me. Since they excelled, my reputation improved and I was seen as a resource in a field outside where I was working.

Having someone as a reference for you means that you are tying your reputation to theirs. A good reference will help you. Your responsibility is to help them. Never make a reference sorry they agreed to be a reference.

Always thank them for being a reference by saying "Thank you" and then out-performing those around you. When you exceed expectations, your reference's reputation is improved.

Researching possible employers

Who would you like to work for? What are they like? Where are they located? What are the names of the companies? Who in the company do you know or could you talk to about a position you would like to have?

The Internet is one of the greatest sources for finding information regarding companies. From finding out what their legal troubles are, to who is employed there, to what they do, and how large they are; you can find out a lot about a company before you apply for a position.

Researching companies can serve you in other ways, as well. It drives me crazy to get a call from a telemarketer who asks what my company address is, when they could have simply checked it out online and asked me to verify the address. This shows that they did not even take the time to find out anything about the company they are calling, before picking up the phone to ask for my business. Don't make the same mistake. Get to know the companies you apply to, and you will be better able to identify how you can help them or how you fit into their organization.

For you, researching potential employers allows you to match your Desired Job against that company. Are they the size you want to work for? Have they been downsizing lately, or are they hiring? What is their company structure? Where are their locations? The better you have defined your Desired Job, the better you will be able to determine whether or not a company is on your list of potential employers.

Using social media such as LinkedIn, you may find that you know someone in the target company. You may also know someone who knows someone in that company. An introduction may be what you need to help you get your foot in the door and a resume into the decision maker's hands.

Most companies have their own web site. If you cannot tell what it is, look at the last part of their e-mail address and see if you can use that to find the site. For instance, the e-mail address: book@HELPsperts.com probably is related to HELPsperts.com or www.HELPsperts.com. This simple lookup will tell you what the company wants you to know about them. You will also see if it has been updated recently, and if you look them up in a search engine you will see what other people have said about them.

Keep track of the information you gather about your potential employers. When you interview with them, having this information will allow you to ask better questions. It says something about a candidate to have them ask "What does your company do?" This tells the interviewer that the candidate did not have the initiative to even do a simple search about the company. A question like "Where do you see the _____ industry going over the next five years?" tells the interviewer that you are thinking long term and took the time to look into the company. A simple question yet provides positive feedback to the interviewer rather than negative.

Looking for a Job

You have identified what type of job you want, you have prepared your resume, and you have researched your possible employers; now how do you find the job you want. You will hear many statistics about how most jobs are never listed on job boards. While this is true, the statistic does not tell the whole story.

You need to keep track of your job search. Imagine sending multiple resumes to the same company. Do you look organized? No. How do you remember when to follow-up when you send out resumes or after an interview? A Job Search Log will keep you organized and help make sure you do not appear disorganized. At the end of this chapter is a sample page from a Job Search Log.

There are several places to look for a job. These places/services include:

- Internet Job Board/Newspaper
- Company Web Sites
- Friends and Family
- Networking
- Social Media
- Recruiters
- Temp Agencies

Each of these places, people, and/or services has advantages and disadvantages. Some charge your new company fees that range from the cost of placing an advertisement (about $25) to three months salary. Others are free to everyone, and still others will charge you, the candidate. Let's take a look at these places to look for a job.

Internet Job Board/Newspaper

There are many job boards available on the internet. These can range from Craigslist.com,[7] which is basically an online classified section, similar to your newspaper (however newspapers all over the US at the same time), to Monster.com,[8] which allows you to place your resume online for companies to review as well as allows companies to place advertisements online for candidates to review.

Job Boards like The Ladders[9] offer a premium service that has fees associated with them. These premium services often include resume review services, resume writing, access to consultants, better placement of your resume with recruiters and companies looking to hire, and newsletters that can help you in your job search.

---

[7] Craigslist.com

[8] Monster.com

[9] TheLadders.com

Most Internet Job Boards are free to the candidate. They make their money from the company paying to place an advertisement or search candidate resumes. Internet Job Boards and Newspapers allow a candidate to look through many potential jobs, very quickly. Internet Job Boards also allow you to save your resume online. This is usually used to either apply for a job or provide potential employers the opportunity to review potential matches, before they even post a job. Many people have found jobs because of these resources.

Job boards such as CareerBuilder.com[10] have excellent articles and tools to use to help you through many aspects of your job search. Their tools tend to be interactive and allow candidates to identify specific job titles you might be interested in, rather than the generalities that are required when writing a book.

On most Internet Job Boards, you can setup specific searches and have the results of these searches e-mailed automatically to you each week. This can save you time each week, searching through a lot of potential jobs.

The downside of using Internet Job Boards and Newspapers is that while you can look through a lot of positions very quickly, there will potentially be a large

---

[10] CareerBuilder.com

number of candidates applying for each position. These applicants can be from anywhere in the world.

A second downside is that whenever you are searching through an Internet Job Board, you must use the job titles they use as well as the terms they list. This can cause issues in several ways. For instance, if you look for a position of IT Manager, you will get a lot of listings for Managers, including Account Managers, Business Managers, Product Managers, and any other position that has Manager in the title. Often you have to put down "Information Technology Manager", in quotes and MAYBE you will have a narrowed response. These boards are getting better; however, due to the rules of searching, it is very difficult for them to narrow your search. Also, if you looked for IT Manager, you might not find the opportunity for Information Technology Manager, or Information Technology Director, or Director of IT. You must use additional terms that may be relevant to the position in order to get all the listings you might be interested in, then you can narrow it down to what you truly want to apply for.

Companies will often have a computer program go through the resumes received (or applications filled out) and rank potential employees by the terms included in their resumes and how well these terms match what was specified for that job. This can be an issue for several different reasons. If you spell a term differently than was setup in a written job description, there may not be a match. For instance, if you said Information Technology, and the person requesting the position called it IT, there would not be a match, even though IT means Information Technology. The reverse is also true. Another issue with computers reading resumes is that the work you put in to format your resume and make sure all of the wording is laid out correctly, is useless. The computer is designed to ignore layout and deal with just the text.

Your actual resume will come in handy when it comes time for an interview, just not during the initial search.

Another issue with using Internet Job Boards is that it can be so inexpensive that other companies will indicate they are looking to hire someone, however when you go in for an interview, you will find that they either are recruiters trying to get a list of names to present to clients, or they are trying to get you to join their organization in a position you are not interested in such as selling insurance or selling financial planning. Unless you are interested in selling insurance or selling financial planning, you should be careful about responding to these types of jobs.

For more information regarding Internet Job boards, please see our web site at HELPsperts.com[11]. Our site has information on sending in your resume for review,

---

[11] HELPsperts.com

the questionnaires in this book, links to other job boards, and information regarding connecting you to the jobs we have become aware of.

In addition to the above sites, your church's web site often has links to jobs that have been made known to them.

Company Web Sites

Many companies list their open positions on their web site. Many have resources similar to a Monster.com where you can setup a login, look for positions, then fill out an application directly online.

If you have done your research, and are knowledgeable about the companies you would potentially like to work for, you should know about their web sites. Since these companies tend to only accept applications from their web sites, this is an excellent way to contact the company. They will often send you information as to what is happening with your application.

The downside of company web sites is that you have to apply to each company individually. Each company also requires you to use a login and password in order to maintain your information. Keeping track of all of your logins and passwords as well as the positions you identified, can often be a daunting task. Use your Job Search Log to keep track of this information.

Friends and Family

Your friends and family are people with a lot of incentive to help you. They care about you and want to see you succeed.

Many friends and family know about positions within the companies they work for and outside those companies that become available. If you communicate with them, often you will find out about jobs before they are listed on job boards.

The key to working with friends and family is communicating exactly what you are looking for. What type of job, where, very general pay ranges (if you are looking for an $80K a year job you do not want them sending you $30K jobs). They will be out looking for what they believe will work for you. The better you help them understand what you want, the better the information they pass to you will be.

Networking

Used properly, Networking is probably the best source of job information and availability.

Every good job I have had has been because of whom I knew, not what I knew. What I knew kept the job.

Networking with people is about what you can do for them, not just what they can do for you. If you focus on what you can do for someone else, it often turns around and someone else, or even that person, does the same for you.

Statistics vary; however, somewhere around 80% of the good jobs never make it to the newspaper or Internet job boards. This means that they are filled by people who find out about the jobs early rather than only looking at job boards. If you want a job, you can either be part of the millions looking at every possibility, identify people who can help you locate a job, or both. My suggestion would always be both.

You have probably heard stories about 100 people applying for one position. If you are going through job boards or newspaper advertisements, you would be one of the 100. If you know someone who walks your resume into the hiring manager for that position, you increase your chances substantially. When you do receive an interview from someone walking your resume into a hiring manager, be sure to remember the chapter on References.

Social Media

With the caveats in the Social Media chapter, social media can get the word out about you, quickly and to people you are already in contact with. Just be sure you do not put anything on a social media site that you do not want your employer to see. Chances are that your current employer as well as your future employers will see whatever is posted by you and about you.

Recruiters

Recruiters are paid to help you. Whether you pay them or the company you will work for will pay them, they make money ONLY when you start working. With this motivation, recruiters have the incentive to help you get the best paying job they can. Before you pay a recruiter, make sure you check their references.

Recruiters tend to be specialized in different fields. Choosing a recruiter in your field can often get you into a job quickly, since they present your resume directly to the decision makers and help guide you through the interview process. They often work directly with the managers of departments as well as Human Resources in order to make sure the candidate (you) are best represented and will work out well.

Recruiters are also in constant contact with companies that are looking for employees, whether or not they are listing the jobs on a job site. They want to help and are always looking for additional candidates to place in positions.

Temp Agencies

Temp Agencies make money putting you to work. When you get hired, they often make money on your placement. Working with a Temp Agency can get you into a company and allow them to get to know you without a long-term commitment. Check out Temp Agencies carefully. Some offer health insurance and other benefits, others do not. Pay ranges vary between the agencies as well.

Concluding Thoughts About Where to Look for a Job
Look Everywhere

While each of the above has positive and negative sides, use any and possibly all of these resources in your search. If you are still employed, you may not want to use a Temp Agency; however, all of the others can work together to help you find the position you need.

Job Search Log

A Job Search Log can be as simple as several pages in a binder that look like this:

Company Name:	
Position:	
Date learned of position:	
Where found out about position:	
Website:	
Login for Website:	
Password for Website:	
Date Resume sent:	
Company contact resume sent to:	
Contact phone number:	
Date of follow-up:	
Type of follow-up:	
Date other information sent:	
Date of Interview:	
Name of Interviewer:	
Type of Interview:	
Date of follow-up to interview:	

Results of Follow-up:

Other information sent:

Key information from interview:

Results of interview and follow-up to interview:

Interviewing

You have identified the job you want. You have sent out your resume (most likely many copies of the resume) and you have been called to interview.

NOW WHAT? This is not a moment for panic, this a moment to be excited about your opportunity to show a potential employer that you are who you said you are, and you are ready, willing and able to accomplish what they need.

The first thing you do is find out about the employer. If you have already researched the company, take that research out and review it. What else is missing? What can you learn about the people you will be interviewing with? Do you know anyone who knows someone at that company? Are there any taboo questions or topics? Are there areas of special interest for those in management? What more can you learn about the company?

When you are researching the employer, check out their web site. Do they have employment information on the site? What about an application?

If they have an application that can be printed out and filled in, you should print it out and fill it in so that when you arrive in the office, you appear even more prepared than other candidates. Almost no-one will bother to look at their company web site and most of them will not have taken the time to fill out an application before arriving.

With your research, you are also looking for questions to ask. If you can find articles written by a member of the company staff, these articles may give you areas where you can ask questions, especially if you happen to interview with the person who wrote the article. If you are not familiar with what the company does, try to identify a few logical and thoughtful questions that will show that you have done your research, but still have questions.

As you are developing your questions, pay attention to the legal issues you find regarding the company. Unless you are interviewing for a position where these issues matter, stay away from them in the interview, however they can be important and you want to be aware of them.

The interview is also your opportunity to interview the employer. You are planning to spend the next 5 or more years with this company and you need to make sure it is a good fit. Designing your questions so that they are aware you are interviewing them as well, can really impress an interviewer.

I once had a candidate ask me, a couple of questions that really impressed me. They included:

- Where do you see the company going in 3 to 5 years?
- Why did you join the company?
- What do you like about the company?
- What keeps you here?

By the time these questions were done, this candidate had a good understanding of what was important to me and what my perspective was. By the way, I hired him as soon as his background check came back clean.

You have completed your research and know what questions you want to ask. It is now just before the interview, what do you need to prepare?

First of all – REVIEW. Review your:

- Resume
- Research
- Job Stories
- Application
- References – call them to let them know you are interviewing and make sure it is ok to use them as references

Second, pay attention to the first impression you will make.

- Clothing – If you are interviewing for an office job, no matter what they have said you should wear, a suit and tie is mandatory for a guy. Be prepared to take off the tie and suit jacket; however, ALWAYS show up "dressed to impress."

- Tattoos – Hide them. In an office environment, there are very few commonly acceptable tattoos. A military tattoo when you have served in the military can be an asset, however almost every other type of tattoo is a liability. This means that if you have tattoos down your arms, you MUST wear long sleeves even in the summer. Tattoos MAY BE acceptable in a field or shop floor environment, however if you aspire to an office or management position, keep them under wraps.
- Smells – If you smoke – Don't! What I mean is, if you smoke, make sure your last smoke before going into an interview is long before the interview, then use mouth wash and a LIGHT body spray to help remove the smell. If you are interviewing with someone that does not smoke or worse yet, quit smoking, the smell of fresh smoke on your clothing can be enough to make them gag. You really do not want their first impression of you to be them gagging. Also, brush your teeth shortly before an interview, and make sure you re-apply deodorant. If possible, shower shortly before an interview. This will help eliminate body odor. DO NOT use perfume, scented body wash

or cologne. Many people are allergic to the scents and some companies have setup rules that you cannot wear scents in an office.

- Hair – If you need a haircut, make sure you have one at least a week before your interview. No matter what you do about a haircut, make sure your hair is neat, brushed, and NEVER in your face. If you typically have your hair hanging in front of your face, make sure it is pulled back, brushed back, or in some other way off your face. Your interviewer wants to interview you, not your hair. Make sure it is not a distraction for you or your interviewer.

- Jewelry – Sedated. On women, an engagement ring or wedding band with a necklace and sedated earrings is perfect. Men, other than a ring, be very careful with ANYTHING ELSE. Many people are old fashioned and not accept other jewelry on a man. No one will expect you to not wear any jewelry; however, nose rings, lip rings, studs in the face or other visible body parts will often turn off the interviewer.

- When it comes to appearance, interviewers are looking for people that will fit into the current company environment. This means that if they think you will be a distraction, they will automatically be looking for something wrong with you or your interview.

Third, the day before the interview, call to verify the time, location, and who you are interviewing with. Sometimes these will change, and it is always better to know for sure.

On the day of the interview, you need to have the following with you when you walk in the door for the interview:

- Your Resume (at least 1 for each person you know you will interview with as well as 1 to 2 extras)
- Application – Sample from earlier in the book or better yet, the one you printed from their web site and filled out.
- References
- A Pen for writing – Make it a nice pen rather than an old office pen.
- Questions to ask
- Positive reading materials about the company
- Paper to write down names of all people you interview with
- General salary range where you could accept a position if it is offered

With everything ready, show up for your interview 10 to 15 minutes before the scheduled interview time. Be prepared to fill out paperwork and to wait for the interview. This wait can be up to an hour. Many companies will have a candidate wait in the lobby for a while to see what they will do. The interviewer may have also had someone show up late for an interview and you are being pushed back just like everyone else will be.

This is a good time to review your resume, questions you want to ask, and the company materials you brought. Fidgeting is NEVER an option. Holding a conversation with other people in the lobby can also be good, however ALWAYS keep it positive. The person sitting next to you may become your new boss. They may also be a competing interviewee.

Write down the names of each person you interview with and the receptionist.

As you are getting ready to leave the interviewer, unless they have already told you, ask what the next step is, and when you should expect to hear from them.

Once the interview is done, immediately mail "Thank You" cards to each of the people you interacted with. This includes the receptionist and interviewer, and whomever you spoke to for any length of time. The "Thank You" card should be purchased at a store and you should hand write a short note inside. Hand write the address on the outside of the envelope.

"Thank You" cards should NEVER be e-mailed.

Why have I spent so much time talking about "Thank You" cards? They are almost a lost art and most likely, no-one else that is interviewing for your position will do it. The card will probably sit on the person's desk after they open it and give them a positive reminder of you. As an example, I received a thank you card from a vendor. After opening it and reading it, it sat on my desk for over 3 weeks. Every time I saw it I thought of her.

Make sure you check your messages, both e-mail and all voice mail/notes/etc., at all locations where the company may have tried to contact you prior to calling about not hearing back from them. It is very embarrassing to find out that someone left a message for you and is waiting for you to arrange another interview. Make sure no-one took a message, wrote it down, and did not give it to you.

The day after you were to hear back from the company, call and speak with the interviewer or leave a message if they are not available. This is simply a message like:

> "You had indicated I might hear back from you yesterday. I am very interested in the position of _____ which I interviewed for, and am looking forward to hearing from you soon. I can be reached at (___) ___-_____. Thank you."

If you have not heard back within two days, sending an e-mail is appropriate. Two days later, calling and speaking with the receptionist to find out when the interviewer might be available and then either calling back when they are available or leaving a message is appropriate.

Touching base by e-mail then phone every two to three days (no more than two contacts a week) until the interviewer responds, is appropriate. Any more often and you will be stalking. If you do not try to contact them, they can assume you are no longer interested in the position.

Second Interview

Depending on how soon the second interview is, you may need to repeat the same steps you went through on the first interview. Most likely, this interview will be with the team with which you will be working. Design your questions around what will be important with that team.

You may also be interviewing with Human Resources. This is the first time you should ask about salary and benefits. Never discuss salary with your team, unless it is directly with your new boss.

Go into the second interview prepared to accept a position if an acceptable offer is presented. You should have discussed salary ranges with your spouse so that you know where to say yes and no and where you might have to consult further. Many organizations will offer a position at this time, and expect you to either accept or reject it immediately.

Keeping Your Job

You now have a job; you have worked really hard to make sure it is what you want, at least for this point in your life. Now, how do you keep it? I have seen several people obtain a job and wind up losing it within a few months. While it sometimes happens that a company goes out of business or hires people and then lays them off, there are often other factors that lead to losing a job.

When you were interviewing for a job, one of the questions you had to answer had to do with gaps in your job history. In order to obtain this job you now have, you must have been able to handle that question, therefore, wouldn't it be nice for this job to not create another gap.

Each company has its own set of rules of conduct. Following those rules will help guide you. On top of those rules, here are some others that have been gleaned from other managers, my experience, and the experience of others.

The first word here is that you need to remember, "You are ALWAYS interviewing for your next job or position." If your boss sees you as someone that can handle their position (appearance, trustworthiness, helping others, etc.) then they can recommend you for a new position. If not, they have other people they can recommend.

Show Up On Time

What time are you used to getting out of bed? That does not matter anymore.

Show up for work so you have got your morning coffee, gone to the restroom, chatted with your co-workers, and are READY TO WORK at the time you are to start. It does not matter what the people around you are doing. You start working (even a couple of minutes early) and you will find that people will notice. Your co-workers may not have positive things to say, however your boss will notice.

This also goes for the end of the day. If you end at 4:00, standing in line to punch out at 3:55 does not work. Put in your full day's work. Again, your boss will notice and will reflect on how hard a worker you are. THIS IS A GOOD THING.

Any time your boss thinks well of you, is great. Anytime your boss thinks badly of you, is an opportunity to lose your job. Keep your boss thinking about you in a positive way. Your bosses' boss may also be watching. I know that one place I worked, if you were still there when the owner left for the day, he specifically said good night to you. Several times, I heard him comment on how hard a worker someone was, because they were working when he was leaving.

Do Your Job

The second rule also sounds obvious, however if everyone would simply do their own job, a lot of companies would run a lot smoother, and a lot of people could complete their own work. When you make a mistake entering information into a computer, do you fix it or do you leave it for someone else to fix? Are you filling out all forms completely and correctly? Many people feel that if they make a mistake, someone else will pick up the slack and fix whatever they messed up.

If you made a mistake, immediately fix it yourself or get in touch with the person responsible for fixing the issue. Always acknowledge your mistake. Do not blame others for what you did. In fact, if you blame others, most people will assume it is because you made a mistake and could not own up to it. If you take ownership, most people will willingly help you resolve the issue quickly, especially if it is their job.

If you cannot finish your job, make sure your manager is aware of what is going on. If they have prioritized something such that you cannot complete your other work, make sure they understand this. Your manager is responsible for making sure you have completed your assigned work. If they have made the decision to reprioritize your time, and you have made them aware of the re-prioritization, they are responsible for handling the discrepancy. If you have not informed them so they can do something about it, it is your responsibility to get BOTH done.

Clothing/Appearance

If you work in an office or visit an office regularly as part of your job, you should always "Dress as if you will be called into the CEO's office." Many offices have minimum dress codes. NEVER go under the minimum dress code.

A word on tattoos and piercings. Unless they are military (and even then if they are too much), always keep them covered. If you have tattoos down to your wrists, you may have to wear long sleeves all the time. Remember what I said earlier, you are ALWAYS interviewing for your next promotion. Tattoos and piercings can be the difference between advancing, staying where you are, and even being let go, whenever there is an excuse.

If you have Casual Fridays, make sure you still dress appropriately. For instance, no matter where you work (even in California) there is no reason to wear blue jeans and a t-shirt in an office environment. Khakis and a polo are business casual. Blue jeans and t-shirt say you are done working for the week and are just showing up to collect a pay check (possibly your final check). If you are moving offices or equipment on a particular day, wearing blue jeans with polo shirt that has the company logo on it is a great way to dress appropriately and still be able to get dirty.

Men should never wear shorts in an office and in most yards, they are prohibited. In the yard, it is for safety reasons, in the office, it is because it is not appropriate business attire. An exception to this would be where you have company dress codes that SPECIFICALLY allow shorts, like UPS or some restaurants.

Women on the other hand have more flexibility on what they can wear, yet their decisions are fraught with risks. Pay attention to how much leg and cleavage you are showing. Some offices appear to not care, however if you are working with other women, even if you wear an outfit only one time, that shows too much (whatever that is in your environment), you may be labeled, or have it talked about for a long time.

One woman I worked with liked to wear clothing that showed a lot of cleavage. She also worked at a desk where if you came up the stairs to enter the offices, she was right there, facing the stairs. You had no choice but to look down her top if you ever wanted to talk with her or even if you were walking past. This made the men around her uncomfortable. There is no reason for anyone to wear clothing like this at work.

If your clothing will make the people around you uncomfortable because of what it shows, leave it at home.

Your choice in clothing also feeds stereotypes about you. While I have met many women who do not fit the stereotype, when you see a tall blond that is wearing an incredibly tight sleeveless top that shows off major cleavage and a pencil skirt, what do you think? For most men, the clothing is a distraction and it is very difficult to take a woman seriously when they choose to dress this way.

Gossip

"If you don't have something nice to say, don't say anything at all." Great advice that you probably give your kids. It is even more important in a business setting. Gossip is easy to get involved in, even if you are not trying to. Getting the reputation for being a "Black Hole of Information" is not a bad thing. In Astronomy, a "Black Hole" is where a star has imploded and now sucks in everything but nothing can get out. In application, a "Black Hole of Information" is the person that you can talk to and know that anything you tell them will NEVER get out.

Becoming known to your boss as the person they can talk to and not have the information go to anyone else, will place you in a great position with your boss. That same boss will be very uncomfortable talking to you about something important, if you then go and talk to the Office Gossip.

The Office Gossip is probably the person who often has a lot of people around their desk, usually for business reasons; whom a lot of people talk to, and that is more than willing to talk about how people shouldn't gossip but "can't understand why Sally is so nice to Bill. There must be something going on." They are often insecure and are looking for validation in sharing their knowledge.

Even as you try to avoid gossip, it will find you. NEVER share it; become that "Black Hole of Information." If you never share gossip, when you do share information, people will respect you and understand that what you say is the truth. They won't question your statements.

If you hear rumors that someone is a gossip. Be careful around them. Your boss has probably heard the same rumor, and everyone who spends a lot of time with people who gossip will become labeled as gossips as well. "Guilt by Association."

Gossip also changes your perception of people. If you hear that "Sally and Bill are having an affair," even if you have every reason to believe it is not true, it can and probably will change your perception of them. The interesting part is that if you think about your perception of the people you heard gossip about, before you heard the gossip, has anything really changed? Probably not. Most likely the gossip was not true, and now you will have to deal with trying to get past that "Knowledge" without creating conflicts.

The best way to keep from having to deal with issues from gossip is to avoid gossip completely. If you are never around gossip your boss and co-workers will realize you are a person that can be trusted.

Respect

You have to EARN respect. Everyone else DESERVES your respect. Show respect to and for EVERYONE, no matter who they are. People notice who shows others respect and they respect this person. As a new employee, part of gaining respect is showing respect.

A little story about earning respect. As a new IT Manager for a company, my first day of work was the day of a flood in the office. A fire sprinkler had leaked in the CEO's office on the second floor and no one realized it for 24 hours. When I walked in, someone had shut off the water but it was still running down the stairs to the first floor. I walked in and started working, unplugging computers and other electronic accessories and handing them to people, directing them where to put equipment and what to take out. It was several hours before I was introduced to my staff and the rest of the office. Over the next week, my department rewired internet connections, phones, power into mobile office trailers, and setup each office person's new space. No business was lost because of the flood, and people got to find out who I was by how I worked. I earned the respect of everyone, by simply getting to work and solving problems in an emergency while showing respect in directing those around me. Gaining respect can come quickly, if you show that you respect those around you and that you are worthy of respect.

A fast way to lose your job is to lose the respect of your boss. When they cannot trust you, they do not respect you. Do not put your boss in this position. Show respect to even the field people who are around you. Show respect to the people bussing your table when you are out to lunch. If you show respect to everyone, you will earn the respect of others.

Learning

Never stop learning. Whenever given the opportunity, learn everything about your job, learn another way to do what you are doing, then learn what your boss does. The responsibility of each boss is to replace themselves. Many do not understand this, however I have had it pointed out to me many times that a person cannot be moved up to a new position until they have trained their replacement. If you have learned your job and are teaching someone to be your replacement, ask your boss what you can do for them or if there is something that you could learn to do that would free up their time. This means you have to make sure ALL of your work is done first; however, the more your boss can see you doing their work, the more likely they will be to trust you with additional responsibilities including being their replacement.

Teaching

If your boss has to train their replacement, so do you. Who is it that is likely to move into your job? Can you train that person or document your job such that someone could walk in and do your job without having to go through a lot of training?

You teaching someone else to do your job actually makes you more valuable to your company. Not everyone can teach others. If you have the ability to learn and then teach someone else, you can move up. You can train your replacement as well as learn other new tasks and help others.

Social Media, Personal Cell Phones, Personal Communications

When you are at work, you are there for business. If you spend time updating your Facebook page, reading your personal e-mails, and talking on the phone to your friends and family, you are stealing from the company. Your time is valuable. The company is paying you to do a job. Even if other people around you are talking on their phones or tweeting, you need to work. When someone does not complete their job on time and you have to pick up the slack, how do you feel if this person is either calling or being called every hour by their boyfriend, wife, kids, etc.? Unless there is an emergency, they are not getting their job done (at least in part) because they are taking care of personal business.

Most businesses allow you to make personal calls on your own cell phone, during breaks. When you walk out of the office for a smoke, every 2 hours, and call someone, your boss notices. If they have to look for you or wait for you, you are keeping them from getting their job done. This shows them that your personal time while they are paying you, is more valuable to you than their time. If your time is more valuable than your bosses' time, maybe you should be working for a different boss.

Never check your social media accounts or e-mails on your company's computers. First of all, anything generated on company computers is the property of that company. Secondly, if you download a virus to your work computer from one of your social media or e-mail accounts, you could lose your job on the spot. Most companies in some way monitor what happens on their computers. Avoiding using them for personal reasons will help you keep your job.

One last point on personal calls. If you cannot be without contact with someone for the amount of time you are working, you need to make sure you set rules of conduct. This means that if your wife needs to call you for something important, they should call and leave a message. My wife and I have an agreement. She calls me when she wants to talk. If I am unavailable (not on a break) she goes to voice mail. If she calls back right away, I will call her as soon as I can. If she calls back a third time, it is an emergency. If there is any way I can answer the call, I do, otherwise I will call her back immediately. I have even informed my boss about that agreement we have.

This allows my wife and me to have communication when needed, however if she is just calling to say "Hi" she can say that to my voice mail and I will pick it up.

Make arrangements with the people in your life that might need to be in touch with you during the day. If there is any way for them to call you after hours, or for you to call them while you are on break, this is best. If this is not possible, make sure that you understand that most companies have a policy about personal calls at work.

Pet-Peeves

Each manager has their own list of pet-peeves. These range from how people should answer the phone, to how people should use e-mails, to whether or not to text customers and vendors using company cell phones. Find out from your manager and those around you, what their pet-peeves are. For instance, some of mine are:

- Leave your ringtone at home. Imagine sitting in a meeting with the CEO of your company, or with a customer, and "Ode To Joy" starts playing from your pocket. How can the other people keep on talking, with a straight face. You have just interrupted the meeting, and I hope it is your wife or husband that called. Use a ringtone that is business appropriate or put your phone on vibrate when you are in the office or in meetings. This pet-peeve may not apply if you are in senior management in a company or senior management has such ringtones, however be VERY careful about this.
- When sending e-mails that are professional, run them through a spell checker. Every e-mail system has one, even on your phone.
- Also, when typing e-mails, DO NOT SEND THE WHOLE E-MAIL IN UPPERCASE LETTERS. This is considered shouting at the person who is reading it. If you do want to emphasize a point, choose where you should capitalize. This is always more effective than SHOUTING.
- Unless you are my boss or my wife, do not send me e-mails that are in text speak. Throwing one lol in the middle of an e-mail is not a big deal,

however do not make me call my kids to have them interpret your e-mail.

- Forwarding Jokes and other junk mail to and from your company e-mail account can cause you to be fired. Many companies track the e-mails coming into and going out of the company. If they see you are mis-using the company e-mail, they can fire you, reprimand you, or simply make it difficult for you to advance. Keep the jokes on your personal account which you do not check at work.
- The subject of many jokes, commercials, and stories is the "Reply All" to an e-mail. This is one of the most dangerous tools you can use. Stories have been told about people who hit "Reply All" and told everyone in their office something that was meant for only one person to see. Send your replys and forwards ONLY to the person or people that need to see the e-mail.
- Pay attention to EVERYTHING in an e-mail before you forward it. If parts of an e-mail are not meant for other people, DO NOT forward it to them. I had an experience where an e-mail where I had replied to my boss was forwarded to his boss, the CEO, who then forwarded it to the whole company. The people reading the e-mail received the full discussion of a topic including who said what, rather than just the

final decision from the CEO. This caused people to come to me regarding the decision that was made by the CEO, even though I had recommended against the decision.

- Do not say ANYTHING in e-mails that you do not want others to know. Many people will forward e-mails without paying attention to everything in them, and not worry about the consequences. If you have stated in an e-mail that you do not like a decision someone has made, and it gets back to that person, you might as well have said it to their face, but even worse, it has gone through a lot of other people first and can cause embarrassment for you and the other person.
- When I make a business call, I expect to hear the name of the person who I am speaking with when the call is answered. Leaving a message at 555-1212 when I don't know if this is the person I am trying to reach, often gets no message from me.
- Respect my time. If you call me and I ask you to call me back because I am busy, call me back when I ask you to otherwise I will not talk with you at all. For instance, when a telemarketer calls me, I ask them to call me back on Friday, any Friday at any time. I am always busy, however I take Fridays to answer this type of call and try to close out my projects for the

week. If the telemarketer calls me on Friday, I will try to answer, unless I am in a meeting or on the phone with another telemarketer. If they call me any other day of the week, I will have them call me back on Friday.

- If you are not my boss, DO NOT text or return personal e-mails from your phone when I am in a meeting with you. If we are at lunch or dinner, that is fine; however, if we are in the middle of a meeting where I am trying to determine how to help you, or you are getting information from me, it is disrespectful. If you are my boss, you are probably at your desk and will be handling business as we are meeting, if you are anyone else, you are indicating to me that your time is more valuable than mine. That may be true, that may not. Do you want to be the person who tells me that my time is not valuable?

These pet-peeves of mine have many exceptions. Certain people, usually the person employing me, are exceptions to these rules. Other exceptions include people who have earned my respect by showing me that they respect me and my time. Emergencies also are exceptions, if I know that there is an emergency, I will do everything I can to help out, even if it means ignoring a pet-peeve

Following these rules will not guarantee you will never lose your job; they will however help you earn the respect of your boss and co-workers.

Conclusion

Looking for a job is hard work. Everyone has thoughts as to what you should be doing and who you should be talking to. In this book I have tried to provide a strategy to follow. There are many strategies. I am not claiming this one is the best, this is designed to take you through a series of steps so you have a logical way to run your search.

Please let me know how you search is going. What steps do you find most helpful? Which did not work?

For additional resources or to contact me, please see my web site at www.HELPsperts.com or e-mail me at book@HELPsperts.com.

Recommended Resources

5 O'Clock Club – FiveOClockClub.com

CareerBuilder.com

Monster.com

Craigslist.com

What Color is Your Parachute? By Richard N. Bolles

Who Moved my Cheese? By Spencer Johnson

HELPsperts.com – Many of the questionnaires from this book are available for free from this site.

Biblical Perspective on Work

This is the part where I get on my soapbox with regard to Christians at work.

The Bible says, "Whatever **you**r hand **finds to do**, **do** it with all **you**r might."[12]

And, "The authorities that exist have been established by God."[13]

This means that those in authority over you were put in place by God and that you are actually representing God when you are working.

If your boss was actually Jesus, when he asked you to do something, would you:

- Roll your eyes?
- Question his right to tell you to do something?
- Talk about his decisions behind his back?

If you said no, then why are you doing that now? If the person in charge was put in place by God, you are actually dis-respecting the person God placed over you, therefore dis-respecting God's decision.

---

[12] Ecclesiastes 9:10

[13] Romans 13:1 b

This is a hard concept to hear. I know for myself, this is an area where I struggle. Part of my struggle is in realizing that even when I am asked to do something that I don't believe God would ask me to do, (as long as ethics and morals are not involved) God IS asking me to do it.

On another topic:

One of the most disappointing things I have heard, from a number of people in several states, is that they hate working with Christians. I find this hard to believe. A Christian employee should:

- Work hard no matter what task is given them. If they are performing the work for God, picking up trash from the front office, or cleaning out the toilet is not beneath them.
- Have a great attitude. There is no excuse for a bad attitude. You work at the job you have because God gave it to you and God wants you there.
- Be the MOST ethical of all employees. There is never a time to put aside ethics, and if you are a Christian, you believe that God is in control. If you lose your job, God will help you find a new one. As a Christian, you understand that your integrity is much more valuable than a pay check.
- Be Courteous to Everyone.

- Respect management. Whether or not you agree with your manager or the company, the Bible calls us to Respect your Elders[14], and Respect those God has placed in authority over you.[15]
- Respect those around you.

As a Christian, you have the responsibility to share your testimony with those around you. What kind of testimony can you have if you say you are a Christian, and are swearing every fourth word or disobeying management? Why should someone want to be like you if they cannot stand to be around you because of your attitude? What kind of testimony do you have?

Your Life is your Testimony. Live your life the way God has called you to live it and people will notice. You don't have to "shove your Religion down their throats." People notice if you are surrounded by swearing and you walk away whenever you can and NEVER swear. Some people will test you to see if they can make you stumble, however most, and even those testing you, are glad to see you succeed.

Remember, you are not alone. One place I worked, I felt I was the only Christian that was trying to lead a Christian life. One day, I found out that the guy that

---

[14] Leviticus 19:32

[15] Romans 13:1-7

worked in the office about 15 feet from me was also a Christian. I later found out that one of my vendors was a Christian, and then found that several people I hired were Christians. God had put many people around to help me succeed and flourish in my walk, and I just needed to trust him and pay attention to those around me.

One of my greatest realizations was when I opened my eyes and saw that God knew what I was going to need, even before I knew about them. God knows what we want, desire, and need and has already prepared for our needs. Often, WE just need to realize our needs.

As you begin your job search, my prayer is that you would first seek God's will and listen for his direction. You have the choice as to what you will do. Make it God's way and you will be much happier than if you fight it.

Remember also, God has the perfect timing in mind. My wife graduated from school in November, top of her class, while raising three kids, trying to keep me in line and being president of at least one organization at my kids' school and involved in several others. She did not find a job in her field until April the following year. In the time she was between school and a job, she was looking every day. I have no idea how many resumes she sent out or interviews she went on. She applied for jobs 45 minutes from home and wound up getting a part-time job about 10 minutes from our house and that will provide additional training. She got better than what we hoped for, and at the same time was able to be there for our kids and their schools, as they went through major productions in music, attended almost every baseball game for my oldest son, and was able to be available for friends and family that had medical issues.

God's timing was to wait. Our timing was to hurry up. God was right. I know that my wife would have been disappointed if she could not have been there for our friends, family, and kids.

God has a plan for your life. It is not necessarily the plan you have. Learn to trust God's plan and you will be much happier than trying to fight God and do everything on your own. As you fill out the enclosed questionnaires, ask God to guide you. Ask others for comments and ideas. Together, you can answer the questions and develop the plan to get you where you need to go. With God's guidance, other people's help, and your perseverance, you can land the job you are looking for.

www.ingramcontent.com/pod-product-compliance
Lightning Source LLC
Chambersburg PA
CBHW051524170526
45165CB00002B/593